Dwight D. Eisenhower

American Leader

T0014430

Curtis Slepian, M.A.

Reader Consultants

Jennifer M. Lopez, M.S.Ed., NBCT
Senior Coordinator—History/Social Studies
Norfolk Public Schools

Tina Ristau, M.A., SLMS
Teacher Librarian
Waterloo Community School District

iCivics Consultants

Emma Humphries, Ph.D.
Chief Education Officer

Taylor Davis, M.T.
Director of Curriculum and Content

Natacha Scott, MAT
Director of Educator Engagement

Publishing Credits

Rachelle Cracchiolo, M.S.Ed., *Publisher*
Emily R. Smith, M.A.Ed., *VP of Content Development*
Véronique Bos, *Creative Director*
Dona Herweck Rice, *Senior Content Manager*
Dani Neiley, *Associate Content Specialist*
Fabiola Sepulveda, *Series Designer*
Dan Widdowson, *Illustrator, pages 6–9*

Image Credits: front cover, p1 Imperial War Museum; p3, p28 MM photos/
Shutterstock; p4 Harry Warnecke/NY Daily News Archive via Getty Images; p5, p19 (top)
PhotoQuest/Getty Images; p10, p24 Bettmann/Getty Images; pp11–13 Corbis via Getty
Images; p14 US Army Signal Corps/Interim Archives/Getty Images; p15 U.S. National
Archives; p16 FPG/Archive Photos/Getty Images; p17 Keystone-France/Gamma-Keystone
via Getty Images; p18 Ullstein Bild Dtl./Getty Images; p20 DOD Photo/Alamy; p21 Daily
Mirror/Mirrorpix via Getty Images; p22 Jerry Cooke/Corbis via Getty Images; p23 A. Y. Owen/
The LIFE Picture Collection via Getty Images; p24 Smith Collection/Gado/ Getty Images
Contributor; p24 Bettmann Archive/Getty Images; p25 Mauritius images GmbH/Alamy;
all other images from iStock and/or Shutterstock

Library of Congress Cataloging-in-Publication Data

Names: Slepian, Curtis, author.
Title: Dwight E. Eisenhower : American leader / Curtis Slepian, M.A.
Description: Huntington Beach, CA : Teacher Created Materials, [2021] | Includes index. | Audience:
Grades 2-3 | Summary: "Dwight David Eisenhower was one of the most important leaders of the
twentieth century. Read about Eisenhower's life in war and peace"-- Provided by publisher.
Identifiers: LCCN 2020043574 (print) | LCCN 2020043575 (ebook) | ISBN
  9781087605074 (paperback) | ISBN 9781087619996 (ebook)
Subjects: LCSH: Eisenhower, Dwight D. (Dwight David), 1890-1969--Juvenile
  literature. | Presidents--United States--Biography--Juvenile literature.
  | Generals--United States--Biography--Juvenile literature. | United
  States. Army--Biography--Juvenile literature.
Classification: LCC E836 .S545 2021 (print) | LCC E836 (ebook) | DDC 973.921092 [B]--dc23
LC record available at https://lccn.loc.gov/2020043574
LC ebook record available at https://lccn.loc.gov/2020043575

5482 Argosy Avenue
Huntington Beach, CA 92649-1039
www.tcmpub.com
ISBN 978-1-0876-0507-4
© 2022 Teacher Created Materials, Inc.

Table of Contents

EISENHOWER USA 8c

Follow the Leader

Dwight D. Eisenhower was a famous leader. He knew how to take charge. People looked up to him. He led the U.S. Army. He also led the country. He was president from 1953 to 1961. His leadership skills helped the country. Many people think of him as a great leader. But how did he become such a strong leader?

General Dwight D. Eisenhower

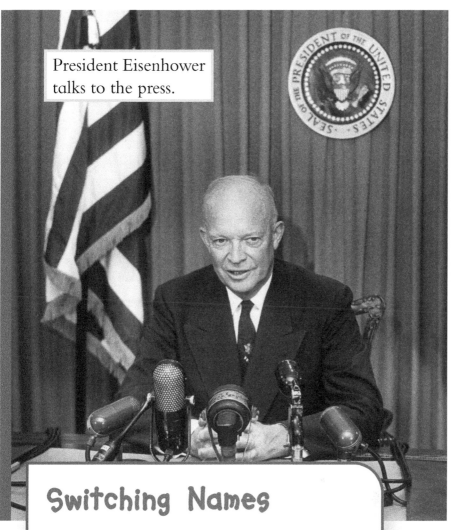

President Eisenhower talks to the press.

Switching Names

Eisenhower was born in 1890 and given the name David Dwight. His dad's name was David too. This was confusing! So, his family changed his name to Dwight David. He also had a nickname, Ike.

Jump into Fiction

Let me tell you a story about Ike. We were in high school in Kansas in 1906. And our football team was in trouble! Our ball was on the 50-yard line. There was time for only one play. I turned to Ike, our captain.

"What's your plan?" I asked in the huddle.

Calm and confident, Ike said, "Let's surprise the other team. I'll throw you a pass."

Naturally, Ike's surprise play worked. I caught his winning touchdown pass!

Ike sure was our leader. He proved it again the next day at school. A new kid arrived in class. Pete was so short that my buddy called him "Shrimp." Guys laughed at Pete. Ike rushed over, angry.

"Leave Pete alone," Ike said. "We shouldn't treat anyone differently."

We were ashamed. But we respected and admired Ike more than ever.

Back to Nonfiction

In the Army

Eisenhower graduated high school in 1909. He worked for two years to help his brother go to college. Then, he went to West Point Academy. The school trained him to become an army officer. But he was not a good student. He wanted to play football.

Eisenhower loved playing football. But he hurt his knee in a game. He could only coach after that. He taught players the value of teamwork. They learned that hard work wins games.

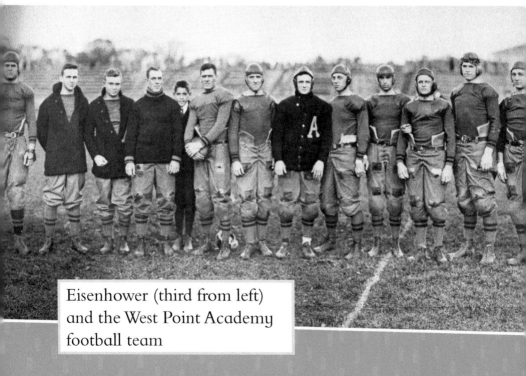

Eisenhower (third from left) and the West Point Academy football team

Eisenhower as a cadet at West Point

Give Peace a Chance

Eisenhower went to a school for soldiers. It made his mother sad. She was a **pacifist**. She was against war.

Eisenhower with his wife and son

The General

Eisenhower graduated from West Point in 1915. Later, he met and married Mamie Doud. They lived on army bases. His job was to train **troops**. He was tough with them, but he was fair. The troops liked him, and the officers did too.

Eisenhower was hardworking and smart. He became a **general** in 1941. Soon after, the United States entered World War II. The war changed his life.

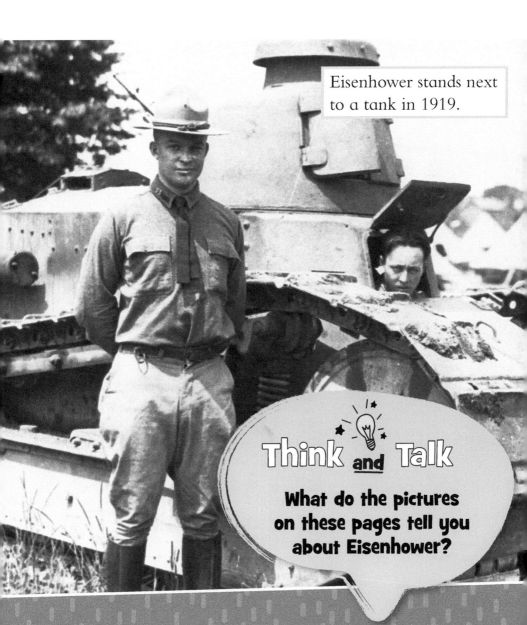

Eisenhower stands next to a tank in 1919.

Think and Talk

What do the pictures on these pages tell you about Eisenhower?

The Big Invasion

During World War II, Eisenhower led the
army in Europe. At one point, they were
mainly in England. Many of the troops there
were from the United States. Some were
from other countries too. Together, they were
the **Allied powers**. They were all fighting
Germany and other **Axis powers**.

Eisenhower works
at his desk.

Eisenhower's job was to help win the war. He came up with a clever idea. He helped plan a surprise attack on the Germans. It worked! The war lasted for one more year. Then, Germany gave up. His plan helped lead the Allied powers to a great victory!

D-Day

Eisenhower's surprise attack is known as D-Day. It happened on June 6, 1944.

Eisenhower gives orders to paratroopers before they launch the D-Day attack.

Eisenhower at Columbia
University in 1948

In Charge

Eisenhower was a war hero! But he chose to leave the army to try a new job. He became head of a university in New York. He was the school's president for five years.

During that time, he was asked to help start a new **organization**. It was called **NATO**. It would help protect and defend the United States and other countries.

But what would Eisenhower do next? Some people said he should lead the country.

General Eisenhower at a NATO Conference in 1951

The President

Eisenhower didn't want to be president. He wanted to focus on NATO. But he thought he could help the nation. So, he ran for president anyway. He won!

United States troops were fighting in the Korean War. Eisenhower thought the country should only be at war if it were in danger. He worked for a **truce**. The fighting ended. The country was not in another war while he was in office.

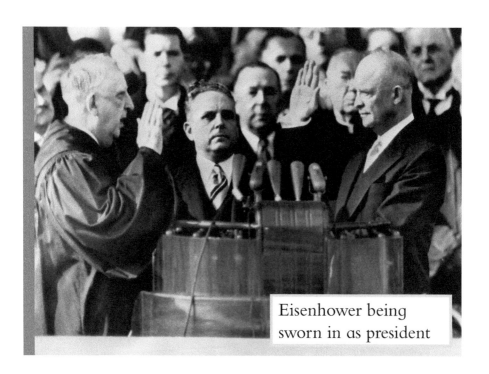

Eisenhower being sworn in as president

Eisenhower visiting troops in Korea

Ad Man

Many **candidates** use TV ads now. Ads tell people why they should vote for them. Eisenhower was the first president to use TV ads when he ran for office.

This giant mushroom cloud was made by a test explosion of an atom bomb.

Peace?

The United States wasn't at war. But it had an enemy. The Soviet Union had taken over many countries. Eisenhower was afraid it would attack the United States. So he had atom bombs built. They could be used to protect the country. The Soviet Union also built bombs like this.

People were worried. Eisenhower said the bombs could be used to bring peace instead of war. But people thought the Soviet Union would attack. He said a war would hurt both countries. The countries did not want that to happen.

The leaders in this cartoon are standing on stacks of bombs.

Think and Talk

What is the artist trying to show in the cartoon?

People liked Eisenhower. He decided to run for president a second time, and he won again! He traveled to many countries and talked to their leaders.

Civil rights were a big issue at the time. So, he signed a law. It said all people should be allowed to vote. But Eisenhower had **critics**. They said he didn't work hard enough to end race problems and **segregation**.

President Eisenhower meets with a leader from the Soviet Union.

U.S. soldiers protect a student arriving at Central High School in Little Rock.

School for All

A school in Little Rock, Arkansas, wouldn't let African American students go to classes there. Eisenhower sent in soldiers to make sure the students were able to go to the school.

Popular President

A new president took office in 1961. The Eisenhowers went to live on a farm. But soon after, the next president asked him for help. Eisenhower was still a great leader. Americans liked him.

Eisenhower had shown leadership skills since he was young. He was calm. He was sure of himself. He was honest. People trusted him. There was a popular slogan when he ran for office. It was "I like Ike." Many people did.

the Eisenhowers at their farm

Honored Leader

There is a statue of Eisenhower in his hometown of Abilene, Kansas. It was put there to honor him as a leader.

Glossary

Allied powers—a group of countries that came together to fight the Axis powers during World War II

Axis powers—a group of countries that fought against the Allied powers during World War II

candidates—people who are trying to be elected

civil rights—the rights that all people should have

critics—people who judge someone or something

general—the highest rank for an army officer

NATO—North Atlantic Treaty Organization, an alliance among 30 countries

organization—a group of people working toward the same goal

pacifist—a person who believes in peace and non-violence always

segregation—the separation of people by race

troops—individual soldiers

truce—an agreement between enemies to stop fighting

Index

Civics in Action

You can be a leader at your school. For example, some students may not know what to do at recess. You can help students at your school make friends and do group activities.

1. Make a list of group activities. Some students might like to run around. Other students might like to sit and talk while doing an activity.

2. List the supplies or equipment needed, such as balls or art supplies.

3. Make and post signs to tell people about the activity you plan each week.

4. Look for students who are by themselves. Invite them to join in!